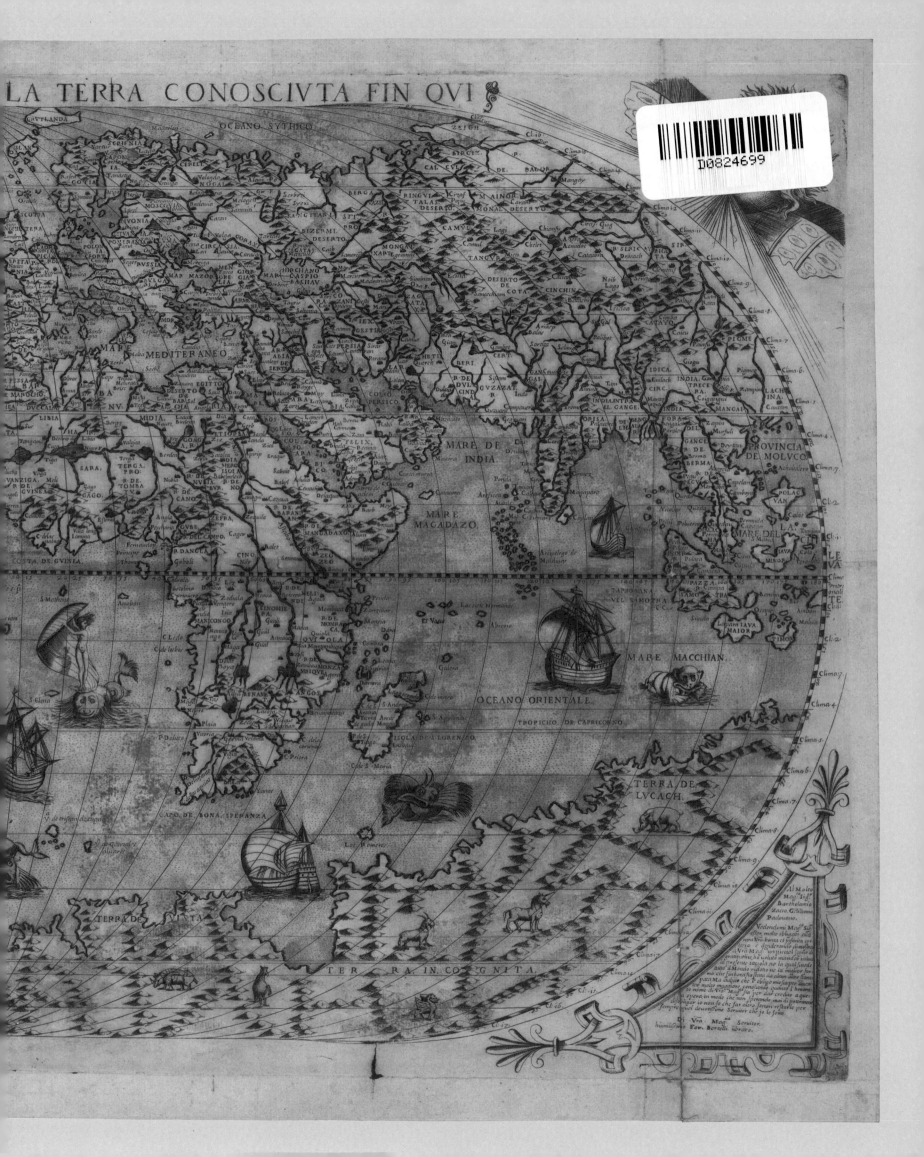

LA TERRA CONOSCIUTA FIN QUI

BUILDING DIPLOMACY

after the terror
looking deeper
into blossoms

—Kristen Deming

Hôtel Pontalba, Embassy Residence, Paris, France

for J. Landis Martin

Through whose sole support this body of work was created
and published and made a gift to the nation

January 2004

Opposite: Palacio Bosch, Buenos Aires, Argentina

Overleaf: Spaso House, Moscow, Russia

ELIZABETH GILL LUI
Photography and Commentary

KEYA KEITA
Cultural Montages

BUILDING DIPLOMACY

Essay by
JANE C. LOEFFLER

with Special Assistance from the Bureau of Overseas
Buildings Operations, U.S. Department of State
KEVIN SPENCE, PROJECT COORDINATOR

An ADST-DACOR Diplomats and Diplomacy Book

Distributed by Cornell University Press
in association with

FOUR STOPS PRESS
Los Angeles, California

Memorial Sculpture, National Museum, Dar es Salaam, Tanzania

DEDICATION

In the name of the victims of violence in the embassy bombings in
Beirut, Lebanon, 1983
Nairobi, Kenya, 1998
and
Dar es Salaam, Tanzania, 1998
I dedicate this book to the building of a public constituency
for the vital work of the Foreign Service
of the United States of America.

Architecture is inescapably a political art, and it reports faithfully for ages to come what the political values of a particular age were. Surely ours must be openness and fearlessness in the face of those who hide in the darkness.
Precaution. Yes. Sequester. No.

—Senator Daniel Patrick Moynihan (1927–2003)

Ottawa, Canada (chancery)

PREFACE

IN THE POLITICAL AND CULTURAL HISTORY OF PLACE, EMBASSIES STAND AS a physical testament to a nation's international engagement. The embassies of the United States provide the indispensable infrastructure by which we deliver America's vision to the world. These halls of diplomacy have borne witness to historic encounters, influential negotiations and the signing of treaties, celebrations of peace and the sorrows of war.

As official representatives of the American people, U.S. embassies are potent symbols in a foreign land. Our presence in these countries is made possible only through the magnanimity of the host country, which has granted us a sovereign place—an American place—within its borders. Our embassy buildings are the concrete evidence of our commitment to international cooperation and provide the stage upon which the vital work of diplomacy goes forward. As long as there is an effort toward peace on this planet, American embassies throughout the world will provide havens for dialogue, opportunities for engagement, and showcases for American ingenuity, design, and technological leadership.

The contributions of artists, architects, designers, and engineers can augment the work of cultural diplomacy in the world. May their creative accomplishments express, with bricks and mortar and quality meant to last, a metaphor for the strength of America's commitment to the building of peace for the twenty-first century.

Elizabeth Gill Lui

Opposite: View of Prague Castle from U.S. Chancery, Prague, Czech Republic

Overleaf: American Legation Museum, Tangier, Morocco

BUILDING DIPLOMACY

Letter from George Washington to the Emperor of Morocco on the occasion of formalizing America's first diplomatic relationship, December 1, 1789

To the Emperor of Morocco
Great and Magnanimous Friend,

Since the date of the letter, which the late Congress by their President, addressed to your Imperial Majesty, the United States of America have thought proper to change their Government, and to institute a new one, agreeable to the Constitution of which I have the honor of herewith enclosing a Copy. The time necessarily employed in this arduous task, and the derangements occasioned by so great, though peaceable a Revolution, will apologize, and account for your Majesty's not having received those regular advices, and marks of attention from the United States, which the Friendship and Magnanimity of your conduct towards them, afforded reason to expect.

The United States, having unanimously appointed me to the supreme executive authority in this Nation, your majesty's letter of the 17th of August 1788, which, by reason of the dissolution
of the late Government, remained unanswered, has been delivered to me. I have also received the letters, which your Imperial Majesty has been so kind as to write, in favor of the United States, to the Bashaws of Tunis and Tripoli, and I present to you the sincere acknowledgments and thanks of the United States, for the important mark of your friendship for them.

We greatly regret that the hostile disposition of those regimes towards this Nation, who have never injured them, is not to be removed on terms in our power to comply with. Within our territories there are no mines either of Gold or Silver, and this young Nation, having just recovered from the waste and desolation of a long war, have not, as yet, had time to acquire riches by agriculture and commerce. But our soil is bountiful, and our people industrious, and we have reason to flatter ourselves that we will gradually become useful to our friends.

The encouragement that your Majesty has been pleased, generously, to give to our Commerce with your Dominions, the punctuality with which you have caused the Treaty with us to be observed, and the just and generous measures taken in the
case of Captain Proctor, make a deep impression on the United States, and confirm their respect for, and attachment to your Imperial Majesty.

It gives me pleasure to have this opportunity of assuring your Majesty that, while I remain at the head of this Nation, I shall not cease to promote every measure that may conduce to the Friendship and Harmony which so happily subsist between your Empire and these, and shall esteem myself happy in every occasion of convincing your Majesty of the high sense (which in common with the whole Nation) I entertain of the Magnanimity, Wisdom, and Benevolence of your Majesty.

In the course of the approaching winter, the national legislature (which is called by the former name of Congress) will assemble, and I shall take care that nothing be omitted that may be necessary to cause the correspondence between our two countries to be maintained and conducted in a manner agreeable to your Majesty, and satisfactory to all the parties concerned in it.

May the Almighty bless your Imperial Majesty, our great and magnanimous Friend, with his constant guidance and protection. Written at the City of New York, the first day of December 1789.

—George Washington

So it was with eloquent and humble words that George Washington embarked his young nation on its journey into a relationship with the world.

One nation-state at a time formally declared its recognition of the burgeoning United States of America until, by 2003, the country could claim some 186 embassies abroad.[1] Yet it was through the good offices of the Sultan of Morocco in 1789 that we first became allied with another sovereign power and set America on its course of finding friends in the world and making something of itself.

Rome, Italy (top, chancery; bottom, residence)

The vision for the role of diplomacy, since the first embassies between city-states were established in Italy during the early Renaissance, was the creation of strength and mutually assured security through peaceful alliances and balances of power. This goal would be achieved through the nonviolent multilateral resolution of disputes. Niccolò Machiavelli was the original author of the idea that nation-states are distinct entities and operate outside the realm of personal morality. He maintained that unlike human individuals who are believed to be capable of altruistic motives, a nation-state will and should act in its own self-interest toward the goal of self-preservation and aggrandizement. Since the Renaissance this concept has maintained a firm hold on the practice of international politics. To facilitate these objectives, resident embassies between nation-states were first established in the mid-1400s, the very first between Mantua and Milan, and have remained since that time the primary conduit through which nations conduct foreign affairs.

As the world's leading democratic republic, the United States has employed numerous approaches to foreign affairs. Throughout our short history, presidents and their advisors have crafted varying philosophies that defined the way in which America interacts with other nations. In the twentieth century, moral criteria have been woven into this evolution in ways that could not have been envisioned during the Renaissance, as they are unique to the American experiment and are inspired by the humanistic principles on which our country was founded.

Faced as we are with even newer realities of international interdependence, an ethical directive for diplomacy in the twenty-first century is emerging. For the peoples of the world to coexist peaceably, the world's leaders are coming to the realization that they must align their national interests with the broader goals of global security and economic stability, which have in the postmodern world become one and the

Kuwait City, Kuwait (chancery)

Ottawa, Canada (chancery)

same. As never before, no nation is an island. National interest in a global society is being reconfigured to encompass the broader interest of the entire human family in security, peace, and justice. The tall order for the work of diplomacy in this century will be to deliver a new vision for peaceful cohabitation of the planet.

Diplomacy is defined as the art and practice of conducting negotiations between nations with the grand objective being peace. In the modern work of diplomacy, peace has come to be viewed as *a process of change toward justice.* This understanding of peace as a process is a very important idea that allows us to continue to work toward its realization even in the face of insurmountable odds and repeated failures. If we do not invest constantly in peace as we go, it will not exist in the background when war is finally eradicated. Is this not how we imagine it: that peace is the stasis and war its disruption?

The embassy of a nation, described in common parlance as the actual building occupied to conduct diplomatic business, is more accurately defined as the mission itself, not its physical apparatus. America's "embassy" to China, for example, is the activity of diplomacy itself. The "chancery" is the building in which the administration of diplomacy is conducted, and the

"embassy residence" is where the ambassador and his family reside and in which many official functions are hosted.

Architecture is the industrialized world's most ubiquitous plastic art and the one artistic medium in which our government has consistently invested. Its significance is enhanced by its integration with mathematics, engineering, and technologies of all kinds. As a cultural export and a tool of diplomacy it reveals much about the achievements and visions of a nation. American identity is reflected in our architectural accomplishments, not only in our embassies but also in the built world we inhabit every day in America.

From the establishment of our first diplomatic mission in Morocco in 1789 through the completion of America's turn-of-the-millennium embassies in Ottawa, Moscow, Kampala, and Kuwait, the history of the U.S. government's overseas building and acquisitions program reflects the epic timeline of America's rise to power. The unique architecture of each embassy conveys a story far beyond that of buildings as ends in themselves. Each of our embassies is one of a kind, a response to the varying factors of politics, time, cultural context, and the history of our relationship with a host country. Expressed through design, architecture, and art—through landscaping

Kampala, Uganda (chancery)

Moscow, Russia (chancery)

Kuwait City, Kuwait (chancery)

Hôtel de Talleyrand, Paris, France

Athens, Greece (chancery)   Ulaanbaatar, Mongolia (chancery)   Palau, Koror, Micronesia (chancery)

and finishes, materials and forms—aesthetics play an integral role in reflecting our self-image to the world. Added to this mix are the powerful influence of American foreign policy and the dynamic and evolving history of our nation's approach to internationalism. Our embassies are multidimensional expressions of values and capacities representative of American culture. Over time that image has shifted and been readjusted in response to political realities. Our embassies tell a story of who we are in relation to the world at any given time and place.

In the course of shooting the images for *Building Diplomacy*, my daughter Keya Keita and I traveled to forty-seven countries between November 2000 and July 2003. We photographed more than one hundred American diplomatic properties chosen as a representative cross section of the types of embassies that America maintains. Throughout our journey into the world of diplomacy, we discovered that although every embassy in the world is unique, they do fall into certain categories. America's commitment to *historic preservation* of properties abroad has been realized in Buenos Aires, Paris, London, Prague, and Tokyo. The rich *mid-century modernist tradition* of buildings built after World War II is showcased

in Mexico, Argentina, Uruguay, India, Indonesia, the Netherlands, United Kingdom, and Greece. *Vernacular buildings* adapted to the demands of a mission are widespread. We photographed examples of adaptive reuse in Mongolia, Ghana, Iceland, Micronesia, and Myanmar. Buildings reflective of *Europe's colonial legacy,* now owned by the United States, are equally in evidence in countries as varied as Argentina, Ghana, Mali, Kenya, South Africa, Tanzania, Zanzibar, China, and Vietnam. *Contemporary embassies* that have been built in the aftermath of violence in Beirut in 1983—called Inman projects, as you will read in Jane Loeffler's essay in this volume —are numerous, including those in Chile, Singapore, Saudi Arabia, Oman, Thailand, Kenya, and Tanzania. The newest embassies, designed since 1998, after the bombings of our embassies in Kenya and Tanzania, are reflective of the security concerns that these events made dramatically clear. Although critiqued for their isolation within walled compounds, it was my observation that they provide some of the highest-quality environments from the standpoint of use by the people who work in them. The embassies in Tunis, Kampala, Ottawa, Nairobi, and Dar es Salaam have been completed, and several more are in the planning and construction phases.

Accra, Ghana (chancery)

Muscat, Oman (chancery)

I have long been interested in the meaning and the metaphor of architecture. The concept that our embassies are a reflection of American identity, and that a building contains unique symbolic potential, had occurred to me in 1991, when Keya and I, after six weeks in economically collapsed Latvia, were guests of Ambassador and Mrs. Jack F. Matlock at the ambassador's residence in Moscow, Spaso House. As I sat there, so grateful to be drinking orange juice from Florida, I gazed at a Milton Avery painting, on loan from an American museum, that hung on a New Empire–style wall and mused how these juxtapositions revealed a story about America and our place in the world. It was years later that the possibility of creating this work became a reality through the generous patronage of J. Landis Martin, a trustee of the Denver Art Museum, a cultural philanthropist, and a connoisseur of art and architecture. With Mr. Martin's support and blessing I was able to approach the State Department with a proposal to document the architecture of American embassies.

With the help of Art in Embassies, the exemplary Department of State program that customizes and installs art collections in embassy residences, my proposal was passed on to the Office of Foreign Buildings Operations (renamed the Bureau

of Overseas Buildings Operations in 2001) and into the supportive hands of head architect Patrick Collins. Patrick and his colleague Kevin Spence, who would become the logistical mastermind of our travels (more professionally called our control officer), skillfully maneuvered us through the hierarchy at the Department of State and successfully obtained the approvals and security clearances needed for Keya and me to actualize this dream.

Planning for the project had begun in the summer of 1999, but our first trip did not take place until Thanksgiving 2000, to Paris, where we shot the renowned Hôtel de Talleyrand on the Place de la Concorde, now used as one of the annexes to the U.S. Chancery. Little could we have known that we would return to Paris a year later to shoot the chancery and the embassy residence, arriving on September 11, 2001. We were in the air over the English Channel when the Twin Towers collapsed. We arrived at the crest of the shock wave that encircled the planet.

At this pivotal juncture in the project (we were about halfway through our intended shooting), we waited anxiously to see if our project would need to be put on hold or even canceled. We were already grateful for all the help that the State

Hôtel de Talleyrand, Paris, France

Department had given us, but became even more so when, with only minor rescheduling, we were able to continue on our way and complete this project. The ramifications of violence had certainly given new relevance to our project and impassioned both of us even more deeply about the significance of the story we were hoping to tell.

THE CREATIVE PROCESS ALWAYS TEACHES AS IT UNFOLDS. In the case of making *Building Diplomacy*, I started with an interest in architecture and art and their potential influence as vehicles for diplomacy. My conviction was certainly strengthened as I maneuvered through the world of diplomacy, yet I was also dramatically reminded that inasmuch as art enlists the timeless, politics drives the immediate. Aesthetic influence may not be the greatest concern in the moment, but it is because we trust in its more enduring aspect that we must diligently employ its humanizing potential in the here and now.

Had it not already been true, the events of September 11, 2001, certainly clarified that the sobering realities of international relations and conflicts enter the mix of issues to be considered when looking at embassies. Beyond the visual

image of beautiful art, or a consideration of architecture, other layers of reality must be factored in, layers revealed by the complexity of the real world and real time. It is in this greatly conflicted world that the work of diplomacy goes forward.

While Americans and world citizens alike question and investigate issues of America's global presence, my hope is that *Building Diplomacy* will contribute to our understanding of who we are at the turn of the millennium by providing a portrait of the official face of American representation on the international landscape. As is appropriate to the social experiment to which we are committed as a nation, individuality and diversity are in wide evidence in the design of our embassies. And yet issues of security have come to dominate the perception of these properties to the extent that even when they are historically significant as architecture, they are described primarily as fortresses or bunkers. The political factors that existed after World War II, which allowed for the openness of modernist architecture as the signature style of embassy design, are as revealing of their time as are today's political realities, which have mandated the fortification of America's missions abroad. At both ends of the spectrum, aesthetics tell a story.

One is justifiably chagrined by the limited access to our embassies imposed by security. Issues become complex when we must balance the value of the work we do with the need to protect ourselves while we do it. It is not unlike the ambivalence we surely feel when we confront the reality of metal detectors in our airports and schools. Violence is a terrible thing and becomes by its nature the cause of many and varied responses. The fortification of our embassies happens to be one of them. The need for heightened security is regrettable, but it is indeed a world fraught with violence and hatred that should evoke our greater disdain. The roots of conflict reflect issues that by and large are external to the world of embassy buildings and their architecture. The work of diplomacy occurs at the heart of conflict, thus by its vulnerability mandates

Great Seal, Ottawa, Canada (chancery)

24

Kuwait City, Kuwait (chancery)

Dar es Salaam, Tanzania (residence)

precaution. As is oft quoted, "more ambasssadors have been killed in the line of duty than have generals."

According to studies of early societies, the building of a *wall* as a companion to agriculture was the first human gesture that separated man and nature. Its psychological significance for human beings is therefore very ancient and very primal. A wall exists to keep bad things out and to protect the good things within. The problem when it is applied to the work of diplomacy, and to education for that matter, is that it may also have the undesirable effect of limiting the open communication and accessibility by which those institutions are defined.

In the seasoned discussion concerning embassies, the wall is perceived as imposing a barrier—if not symbolically, then definitely practically—to the effectiveness of diplomatic work, which from an American values perspective should exude openness, accessibility, transparency, and receptivity. If the wall communicates the opposite by its physicality and its psychology, then we must ask if its presence is antithetical to the inherent nature of diplomacy. This is the basis for concerns about the impediments of security in the context of the work of diplomacy.

There have been long and strenuous debates over the restrictive access that containment imposes on our embassies. Since the bombings of the U.S. Embassy and Marine barracks in Beirut in 1983, many conscientious and esteemed lawmakers and policy analysts from both public and private sectors have engaged in this discussion. Senator Daniel Patrick Moynihan will be especially remembered as a passionate advocate for meeting these challenges with vision and balance. The extreme loss of life in the bombings in Nairobi and Dar es Salaam renewed the focus on these issues and risks, resulting in the current proliferation of new embassy construction and renovation. Since embassy design is far ahead of the learning curve with regard to security, 9/11 did not create a new awareness so much as it reinforced and validated the pressing need we have as a nation to ensure the safety of Americans.

Following the demise of the Inman program in the 1990s the State Department initiated very few new construction projects until the 1998 embassy bombings in Africa prompted additional funding for security upgrades and the construction of secure embassies and consulates. After the 1998 attacks, the State Department identified 185 existing embassies and

Nairobi, Kenya (chancery)

consulates worldwide that would need to be replaced to meet security standards.

To address security shortcomings, the State Department in 1999 embarked on an estimated $21 billion embassy construction program, the largest of its kind in the Department's history. The program to replace diplomatic properties is in its early stages, but the pace of initiating and completing new projects has accelerated significantly since the 2001 attacks on the Twin Towers and the Pentagon. As of September 2003 the Bureau of Overseas Buildings Operations had begun the design and construction of twenty-two projects to replace facilities at risk of terrorist or other attacks.[2]

All that being said, despite increased security, any U.S. citizen who needs help from an American embassy, for whatever reason, will find ready and willing assistance by simply making a phone call or walking up to the front gate with an American passport. Although our properties are not as open as a city park, a cultural institution, or a public library, they are seen and enjoyed by many people who for a variety of reasons have business to transact with the embassy, the principal beneficiaries being American citizens traveling overseas. Our government has an established international infrastructure

that will come to the aid of any American, anywhere in the world. If you can travel there, more likely than not our Foreign Service will be there to assist you.

Embassies also serve, which is their primary function after all, as places where the U.S. government carries out its business with and in foreign countries. Despite impressions from the street, the buildings are active and busy environments. Many foreign nationals are employed at our embassies around the world, more so than Americans. The dedication of these foreign employees is epitomized by the Afghanis who, without compensation, protected our embassy in Kabul during the years the country fell under Taliban rule. Many other foreigners and Americans have active working relationships with our diplomats, and many conduct business within the embassy itself. A primary role of diplomacy is to facilitate America's economic and trade interests, and to this end embassies dedicate considerable effort. In all of these aspects, the success of the mission of the embassy can be greatly enhanced by the highest professional standard of quality expressed through its physical environment.

There is no denying that security has in some cases imposed damaging effects on the aesthetic integrity of our embassies.

Accra, Ghana (former chancery)   Singapore, Singapore (chancery)

One feels true regret when looking at a crumbling gem of a building such as Harry Weese's chancery in Accra, Ghana, decommissioned as an embassy because it was determined that it could not be secured. Now owned by a Ghanaian women's organization, it stands forlornly rotting on its elegant modernist *pilotis*, waiting desperately for the monies needed to restore it. The current challenge of securing embassies such as Eero Saarinen's chancery in London, or the proposed Moore Ruble Yudell chancery in Berlin, both on culturally significant historic sites in tight urban settings, is certainly problematic, and aesthetics and design may be compromised without even achieving the ultimate security solution. Yet on the other hand, one feels extreme pride when standing in the atria of chanceries such as those in Ottawa or Riyadh or Moscow, marveling at the successful integration of aesthetics with the engineering of such a technologically advanced and secured building type.

While shooting *Building Diplomacy*, I came to believe that the need for security around the periphery of our embassies, although imperative, is definitely only one aspect of these properties and not one to which all other dimensions of diplomacy should be sublimated. Innovative and excellent

architectural firms have approached the design and integration of permanent barriers, secured setbacks, and counterterrorism devices with evenhandedness and a concern for aesthetics. As Gale Ruff, our control officer in Singapore, told us when we asked him if he liked the building, "What's not to like? It's an engineering masterpiece." And yes, there is still a highly secured perimeter surrounding this twenty-first-century marvel. Admittedly, the more temporary solutions put in place in the aftermath of 9/11, such as barricades and armored vehicles, project a daunting impression of our embassies. Whether permanent or temporary, seen as successful or damaging, these measures reveal much about the times in which we live.

TRAVELING THROUGHOUT THE WORLD VISITING MANY of our diplomatic missions has been a privilege and a life-changing experience for me as an artist. This book is truly only one manifestation of the multiple dimensions of that experience. I have had many revelations and drawn many conclusions, but above all I have become even more impassioned about the unlimited potential for an expanded definition of diplomacy, for employing the soft power of the creative in order to heal and teach and transform, and for embracing a broad cultural activism at home and abroad.

Until the day when we fully engage the arts, the sciences, and the humanities in their ability to transform human thinking and values, we will succumb to control by the cruder forces of violence, egotism, and ignorance. We must enlist as our tools of diplomacy all possible humanitarian initiatives meant to eradicate disease, poverty, and ignorance and to support health, economic stabilization, education, and the preservation of culture. Such initiatives lay the foundation for a new world paradigm supportive of mutual understanding, cooperation, and respectful coexistence.

A far more concerted investment in the cultivation and export of the best that America has to offer can certainly contribute to shifting world opinion toward us more favorably. With comprehensive and concentrated diplomatic initiatives, we are investing not only in international goodwill but in the broader goals of securing stable global markets and opportunities for American trade and economic prosperity. Our nation should commit to a robust initiative in the employment of the many and varied tools of diplomacy, including great art and great architecture. All means must be enlisted in the effort to share the humanity of who we are as a people, our accomplishments, and our aspirations.

In addition to these efforts, America has the opportunity, through the existing infrastructure of our embassies, to contribute to the preservation of other cultures around the globe, be they in Mongolia, Monaco, or Micronesia. The preservation of the wealth of our planetary diversity is the respectful counterpoint to promoting what we choose to share of ourselves. For all governments, an expanded definition of diplomacy would facilitate the realization of these objectives. The tools of diplomacy can become exhausted only if we limit the means we employ toward these ends.

Buenos Aires, Argentina (residence)

Jane C. Loeffler

EMBASSY ARCHITECTURE AS POLITICS AND SYMBOL

As a tangible expression of America's official overseas presence, our embassies have always played a key role in our diplomatic history, but oddly enough, that history is generally told with little or no reference to the actual buildings themselves. Likewise, embassies have figured significantly in the history of U.S. architecture, but accounts of that history pay little attention to these faraway landmarks, although many were designed by leading American architects and contributed to the architects' professional development. Americans readily identify courthouses and capitols as public buildings, but most would not think to add embassies to that group. "Out of sight, out of mind" is an adage that may help to explain why embassies have been so frequently overlooked by historians and why they are so misunderstood by the general public and by elected officials. What follows is a brief history of the U.S. foreign building program, underscoring the importance of embassies as potent symbols of international commitment.

The first envoys sailed to Europe just after the American Revolution to represent U.S. interests and solidify support for the new nation. In Paris, London, Madrid, and Lisbon, they procured their own dwellings depending on what best suited their pocketbooks. One exception was the Tangier legation, a spacious white-washed house with an open courtyard, a tile roof, and ornate Moorish arches. It was a gift to the U.S. government in 1821 from the Sultan of Morocco and became the first official U.S. diplomatic property.

Congress did not deem it necessary to provide its overseas representatives with living quarters or office spaces until 1911, when persistent outcry from American businessmen, embarrassed by comparisons between U.S. facilities and those of other nations, resulted in the passage of the Lowden Act, legislation that enabled the U.S. government to buy property abroad for the first time. The Schoenborn Palace in Prague was one of the first major purchases (1925). With its panoramic view of the Prague Castle, the seventeenth-century Baroque palace gave the United States a high-visibility presence in the Czech

Stockholm, Sweden (chancery)   Kuala Lumpur, Malaysia (chancery)

Montevideo, Uruguay (chancery)   Accra, Ghana (chancery)

Athens, Greece (chancery)

The Hague, Netherlands. Flower offerings in memory of the victims of September 11, 2001.

accessible sites as near as possible to key government buildings; and many, such as those in Athens (The Architects' Cooperative, Walter Gropius, 1959) and Mexico City (Southwestern Architects, 1961), featured open courtyards. With designs that welcomed the public and provided open access to U.S. books, newspapers, films, and an array of cultural programs, embassy architecture of that era was hailed as an apt expression of American values, and nearly everyone associated with the foreign building program endorsed the evident relationship between visual openness and democratic ideals.

Two circumstances in the early 1960s caused the building program to shift its emphasis. First, once credits were no longer available as a funding source, members of Congress sitting on key oversight committees started to use their political muscle to determine what was built as well as when and where. Thus, Ohio Democrat Wayne Hays was able to block plans to build a new embassy in Dublin for years, claiming that John Johansen's circular glass-and-concrete design resembled a flying saucer or a pile of flapjacks, and he was also able to veto plans to build needed embassies in newly independent African nations that he considered to be unreliable allies.

Second, by the mid-1960s, embassy security was becoming a growing problem. Before that time, the main concerns were fire, theft, and espionage. When vandals threw rocks at the glass walls of the consulate in Frankfurt in the 1950s, they were dismissed as a nuisance. Even when 10,000 Bolivians stoned the U.S. Embassy in La Paz in 1959, it was considered an isolated event. But once the Viet Cong attacked the U.S. Embassy in Saigon in 1965 and three people died, the State Department added defensibility to its design strategy. FBO focused first on perimeter security—gradually adding fences, planters, and bollards to control pedestrian access and prevent vehicles from approaching embassy buildings. At the same time, it hired fewer "big name" architects, and new designs reflected a policy that was more functional than artistic. One example of this new utilitarian design is the chancery in Nairobi, designed by A. Epstein & Sons in 1971.

Control of public access is more evident in Frederick Bassetti's design for Lisbon (1983), where spiked rails were built into each window bay, and in the Hartman-Cox design for Kuala Lumpur (1983), described to me by George Hartman as a "concrete pillbox broken down to resemble a house." In the early 1980s, while these projects were under construction,

FBO sent architect Harry Weese back to Accra to see if his chancery there could be retrofitted to meet security standards. With its open ground floor, its single entrance/exit staircase, and its heavy wooden shutters, the building no longer met minimal standards and was subsequently abandoned. By that time, architects were no longer using *pilotis*, glass walls, (climbable) screens, and other features that were once so popular.

When terrorists bombed the U.S. Embassy and Marine barracks in Beirut in 1983, FBO halted plans for new construction while experts assessed the damage. Projects in Riyadh (CRS Sirrine, 1986) and Muscat (Polshek Partnership Architects, 1989), already under way, proceeded with modifications. Admiral Bobby Ray Inman's report on the Beirut bombings (1985) called for the construction of scores of new embassies and the abandonment of dozens of existing buildings, and it strongly recommended locations far from downtown areas, with residences and offices combined on a single site that could be surrounded by a 9-foot-high reinforced concrete wall. The report also called for a minimum 100-foot setback from vehicular traffic, increased use of electronic locks and surveillance systems, and interior barriers, or "hard lines," designed to thwart intruders. The new standards had a profound impact on embassy architecture, but FBO was determined not to allow security enhancement to interfere with overall design quality. The first of the so-called Inman projects was the U.S. Embassy in Sanaa, designed by CRS Sirrine as a walled compound on the city's outskirts (1990). Others followed in Amman (1992), Nicosia (1993), Pretoria (1993), Santiago (1994), Caracas (1995), Bogotá (1996), Kuwait City (1996), Lima (1996), Bangkok (1996), and Singapore (1997). Architect Leonard Parker described the difficulty of creating an inviting building for Santiago when limited to a 15 percent window/wall ratio. He used rooftop skylights to bring light into the relatively windowless interiors and rich-looking materials as a contrast to a relatively severe exterior.

Riyadh, Saudi Arabia (chancery)

Pretoria, South Africa (chancery)

Santiago, Chile (chancery)

Kuwait City, Kuwait (chancery)

Lima, Peru (chancery)

Bangkok, Thailand (chancery)

Singapore, Singapore (chancery)

Dar es Salaam, Tanzania (chancery)

Kampala, Uganda (chancery)

Arquitectonica faced a similar problem at Lima when the embassy moved from a location on a busy downtown street, where it had come under guerrilla fire, to a larger and more protected suburban site. The architects took their cue from the distant Andes Mountains, designing a colorful patterned façade dotted by real and imaginary windows that reads as environmental art.

By the mid-1990s, memories of Beirut had faded and the State Department granted waivers from the Inman standards, recognizing that it could not and should not apply the same standards at all posts worldwide. In Ottawa, for example, a scheme had been abandoned in 1983 because its prestigious downtown site near Parliament Hill did not provide adequate setback from adjacent streets. After a search for a suburban alternative, however, the Department decided on the first site in order to maintain a high-profile U.S. presence in the Canadian capital (comparable to Canada's in Washington) and to underscore U.S. trust in its northern neighbor. In 1994, FBO retained David Childs of Skidmore, Owings & Merrill to design the new Ottawa chancery. One year later, when a bomb destroyed the federal office building in Oklahoma City, Childs significantly upgraded the security of the proposed

chancery by moving the atrium to the interior and inserting a concrete blast wall behind the west-facing glass façade. The chancery opened in 1999. It is significant not only for its accessible location but also for a design that features two different façades, each reflecting the disparate surroundings: the glass-walled National Gallery of Canada on one side, and the historic market district on the other. The embassy also boasts a remarkable art collection. Its most visible piece is Joel Shapiro's forty-foot bronze sculpture *Conjunction*, which stands at the building's south end.

Balancing openness and security was the greatest embassy design challenge long before terrorists bombed U.S. embassies in Nairobi and Dar es Salaam in 1998. In the aftermath of those events, the State Department reassessed risk and moved ahead quickly with plans to rebuild chancery compounds in or near both capitals. Designed by HOK/Washington, both opened in early 2003. The vulnerability of posts in the region also prompted the Department to expedite completion of the new embassy compound in Kampala, which was designed by RTKL Associates (2002).

With plans under way to build new embassies in Tbilisi (Georgia), Dushanbe (Tajikistan), Phnom Penh (Cambodia),

Ottawa, Canada, U.S. Chancery with Joel Shapiro sculpture, *Conjunction,* 1999. Gift of Friends of Art and Preservation in Embassies.

Moscow, Russia (residence)

Tashkent (Uzbekistan), Kabul (Afghanistan), Beijing (China), and elsewhere, the United States faces the increasingly difficult challenge of providing its foreign representatives with safe and suitable workplaces and residences. While Congress and the administration react swiftly with promises of support when disasters occur, those promises do not always turn into dollars, and increasingly large portions of proposed funds are earmarked specifically for security. Such funds cannot be spent on sorely needed maintenance or on other necessary improvements. Thus, generous-sounding funding packages may represent risk aversion more than a real recognition of the role that embassies play as billboards for American values. Moreover, it would be a mistake to interpret an embassy security budget as evidence of a commitment to architectural excellence.

Elizabeth Gill Lui's photographs assembled here provide a glimpse of what it means to try to find a way to establish a

dialogue with the world around us. They are especially timely as debate rages about the nature of American identity, because as history has shown, a nation projects its identity through its public buildings. The photographs provide unique access to doorways, courtyards, hallways, reception rooms, offices, and gardens that the general public will never see because of the layers of security that now put U.S. embassies off-limits to most would-be visitors. Although infrastructure is only one component of diplomatic representation, the relative isolation of U.S. embassies, particularly the newest ones, adds to the challenge of establishing an effective foreign presence. A strong commitment to public diplomacy and a renewed emphasis on cultural exchange would be one way of bettering our image abroad. Historically, at least, we have explained democracy and celebrated American individuality through architectural and artistic achievement. Now is the time for more of that, not less.

Prague, Czech Republic (residence)

Western Hemisphere

featuring

Buenos Aires, Argentina

Montevideo, Uruguay

Santiago, Chile

Lima, Peru

Mexico City, Mexico

Ottawa, Canada

Chancery
1970
Eduardo Catalano
Architect

PALACIO BOSCH

Palacio Bosch, built between 1912 and 1917, was designed by French architect René Sergent for Ernesto Bosch and his wife, Elisa de Alvear. After representing his country in Germany, the United States, and France, Bosch became Argentina's Minister of Foreign Affairs in 1910. André Carlhian, a specialist in traditional French classicism, was responsible for the interiors. Achille Duchêne designed the garden with its sophisticated geometry. The façade, in the style of Louis XVI, echoes the small temple that stands opposite in Palermo Park. Grand interior rooms, arranged around a central loggia and staircase, overlook the garden. The building was seminal to Argentine architectural taste. Because of its stylistic unity and contextual relation to its environs, this residence is considered to be among Sergent's finest works.

Bosch sold the residence to the U.S. government in 1929 following recurrent propositions by U.S. Ambassador Robert Wood Bliss, who had appealed to President Herbert Hoover to support the purchase of a property that would project an image of architectural prestige in a prominent location in the Argentine capital. Bliss's discriminating taste in architecture and art is further in evidence at Dumbarton Oaks, the home and gardens he built in Washington, D.C. With the professional guidance of leading American and Argentine experts on historic preservation, an extensive renovation of Palacio Bosch was completed in 1999 by the Department of State's Office of Foreign Buildings Operations. The Palacio Bosch is a designated historic landmark by the Buenos Aires municipality and the Argentine Republic.

Residence
PALACIO BOSCH
1917
René Sergent
Architect

Chancery
1969
I. M. Pei
Architect

Chancery
1994
The Leonard Parker
   Associates
Architects

Chancery
1996
Arquitectonica
Architects

Residence
1945
Office of Foreign Buildings Operations,
    U.S. Department of State

There can be no greater good than the quest for peace,
and no finer purpose than the preservation of freedom.

—Ronald Reagan
United States Congress
Geneva Summit Meeting
November 21, 1985

Chancery
1961
Southwestern Architects

65

Residence
1964
Carlos Reygadas
Architect

Chancery
1999
Skidmore, Owings & Merrill (SOM)
Architects

Monument to Canadian Peacekeeping Missions,
adjacent to the U.S. Chancery.
Jack Harman, 1992

Residence
1908
Built for Warren Y. Soper
Ottawa Electric Company

Africa

featuring

Pretoria, South Africa

Accra, Ghana

Bamako, Mali

Dar es Salaam, Tanzania

Stone Town, Zanzibar

Nairobi, Kenya

Kampala, Uganda

Chancery
1993
Eduardo Catalano
Architect

Residence
HILL HOUSE
1940
Burg Lodge & Burg Architects

Currently the property of the Ghanaian government, America's former chancery remains in need of the funding required for its restoration. A women's organization in Accra has hopes of transforming the building into a health and education center for the benefit and welfare of women and children.

Former Chancery
1959
Harry Weese
Architect

Human rights are the soul of our foreign policy, because human rights are the very soul of our sense of nationhood.

—Jimmy Carter
Ceremony commemorating
the 30th Anniversary of the
United Nations Declaration
of Human Rights
The White House
December 6, 1978

Chancery
1972
Regional vernacular

Chancery
2003
HOK/Washington
Architects

a tree planted
to remember them by—
deepening shade

—Kristen Deming

*Traditional carved doors by renowned Tanzanian carver
Munir Salim Omar. Design motif depicts aspects of the
various races and cultures that make up Tanzania and
Zanzibar. Gift to the U.S. Embassy from the Tanzanian
government in commemoration of the embassy bombing,
August 7, 1998.*

Chancery
2003
HOK/Washington
Architects

ZANZIBAR'S DIPLOMATIC CONSULATES

Zanzibar, an island off the coast of east Africa with a rich multicultural history, was the home to one of America's earliest diplomatic consulates. Zanzibar was a significant port on the trade route from Asia and India to Europe and the New World and a protectorate of Oman throughout the nineteenth century. Omani Sultan Seyyid Said moved his capital from Muscat to Zanzibar in 1837, at which time he established Zanzibar's first treaty with a foreign country by entering into a commercial and trade relationship with the United States. This treaty predates Zanzibar's official recognition of Great Britain and was influential in enabling the United States to curtail and eventually outlaw the slave trade that once thrived on the island.

The building first occupied by the U.S. Consulate is the present Tembo Hotel (above), on the seafront next to the Old British Consulate. The coastal locations of each of these historical proper-ties enabled the docking of trade vessels at the consulates' doorsteps. The more recent building to serve as home to our diplomatic mission is a 1930 two-story structure of modern design (opposite). Its open balcony is a departure from Zanzibar's traditional Islamic-style architecture, which always had enclosed balconies to protect the females of the household from view. As there is no record of the United States having owned either of these properties, it can be assumed that they were leased from the Zanzibar government.

The United States' mission on Zanzibar was elevated to the status of an embassy when Zanzibar achieved independence on December 10, 1963. Upon the unification of Zanzibar and Tanganyika, on April 26, 1964, the mission was once again designated a consulate, now to the newly renamed nation of Tanzania. The consulate was officially closed in 1978, at which time ongoing diplomatic business became the responsibility of the embassy in Dar es Salaam.

Chancery
2003
HOK/Washington
Architects

Chancery
2003
HOK/Washington
Architects

The pursuit of peace and progress cannot end in a few years in either victory or defeat. The pursuit of peace and progress, with its trials and its errors, its successes and its setbacks, can never be relaxed and never abandoned.

—Dag Hammarskjöld
United Nations Secretary-General,
1953–1961
Nobel Peace Prize, 1961

Staff Housing Compound
Completion, 2004
Beglin Woods Architects

Chancery
2002
RTKL Associates
Architects

Near East and South Asia

featuring

Tangier, Morocco

Casablanca, Morocco

Tunis, Tunisia

Cairo, Egypt

Muscat, Oman

Riyadh, Saudi Arabia

Kuwait City, Kuwait

New Delhi, India

American Legation Museum
1821
Regional architect
Gift of the Sultan of Morocco

TANGIER OLD LEGATION

The Tangier Old Legation, the first property acquired by the U.S. government for a diplomatic mission, was presented in 1821 as a gift to the American people by Sultan Moulay Suliman. His generosity was inspired by the success of the Moroccan-American Treaty of Friendship. This 1786 treaty, with John Adams and Thomas Jefferson as signatories, was renegotiated by John Mullowny in 1836. Still in force today, the treaty is among the most durable in American history. The Cape Spartel Lighthouse Treaty of 1860, which was negotiated in the Old Legation, is considered to be the forerunner of the League of Nations and United Nations because it speaks to broad cooperation within international law.

Located within the ancient city walls, the legation compound was enlarged during 1927–31. From the upper terraces there is an incomparable view of the harbor and Straits of Gibraltar, and, on a clear day, of Gibraltar and the Spanish towns of Allegories and Tarifa. The complex is a harmonious blend of Moorish and Spanish architectural traditions. When the consulate general moved to another location in Tangier in 1961, the property became an Arabic-language school. Since 1976 the compound has been leased to the Tangier-American Legation Museum Society. The museum maintains a collection of engravings, maps, rare books, and works of art by many American artists who have lived in Morocco; the complete archives of the writer Paul Bowles are included.

The library is located in a separate three-story building of 18th-century origin now attached to the museum. With its central atrium, exposed wood-timbered ceilings, and Moroccan decor, the research library is one of the most traditional sections of the museum.

The Legation Museum is dedicated to honoring the history of more than 200 years of U.S. and Moroccan diplomatic relations.

Residence of the
  Consul General
VILLA MIRADOR
circa 1920
Regional architect
House where Winston Churchill
  stayed during the Casablanca
  Conference, 1943

Residence
1974
Brahim Taktak,
   with John Marmey
Architects

View from terrace across Bay of Tunis with view of the twin peaks of Bou Kornine.

Chancery & Residence,
    Phase I
1982
Metcalf & Associates
Architects

Chancery, Phase II (left);
    Phase I (right)
1987
The Architects' Collaborative
    (TAC)
Architects

Chancery
1989
Polshek Partnership
  Architects

Residence
1990
Ayoub Oghanna Associates
Architects

Chancery
1986
CRS Sirrine
Architects

Residence
1986
CRS Sirrine
Architects

Chancery
1996
RTKL Associates
Architects
Gift of the Kuwaiti government

Residence (left)
1996
RTKL Associates
Architects

Staff Housing (right)
2002
Sorg and Associates
Architects

The defense of freedom is firmly grounded in an appreciation of its value. No government, no foreign policy, is more important to the defense of freedom than are the writers, teachers, communication specialists, researchers—whose responsibility it is to document, illustrate, and explain the human consequences of freedom and unfreedom.

—Jean Kirkpatrick
United Nations
Committee for the Free World
January 23, 1982

Chancery
1959
Edward Durell Stone
Architect

East Asia and Pacific

featuring

Tokyo, Japan

Seoul, South Korea

Ulaanbaatar, Mongolia

Beijing, People's Republic of China

Shanghai, People's Republic of China

Manila, Philippines

Hanoi, Vietnam

Rangoon, Myanmar

Bangkok, Thailand

Jakarta, Indonesia

Kuala Lumpur, Malaysia

Singapore, Singapore

Canberra, Australia

Chancery
1978
Cesar Pelli with Gruen Associates
Architects

AMBASSADOR'S RESIDENCE

In 1925 the United States acquired the site of the ambassador's residence in Tokyo from the Japanese government for $115,000. Formerly the estate of Prince Ito Hirokuni, son of Japan's first prime minister, the Prince's residence, along with the adjacent U.S. Embassy buildings, had been destroyed two years earlier by an earthquake and subsequent fire. American H. Van Burren Magonigle and Czech-born Antonin Raymond were commissioned to design both a new residence and a chancery. Raymond, who had come to Tokyo to work for Frank Lloyd Wright on the Imperial Hotel, employed principles of Japanese philosophy in the design and orientation of the building as a means of providing for the harmony and well-being of its occupants.

The residence is a blend of Moorish and Asian stylistic influences with colonial overtones. Its spacious reception rooms and large garden offer uncommon serenity in the center of downtown Tokyo. This residence was among the first houses built by the United States specifically as an ambassador's residence and was one of the first projects of the new Foreign Service Buildings Commission set up by President Herbert Hoover. Dubbed "Hoover's Folly" at the time, the chancery and the residence, with imported Georgia walnut wall panels and Vermont marble flooring, were completed during the depression at a cost of $1.25 million dollars.

During World War II the compound was under the protection of the Swiss government. From 1945 to 1951 General Douglas MacArthur lived in what his staff called "The Big House." On September 27, 1945, Emperor Hirohito came to the residence to acknowledge his nation's surrender to MacArthur. The next day a photograph of their meeting in the living room was printed on the front page of every newspaper in Japan. It conveyed the new position of Japan's "living god," for by subordinating himself to MacArthur, Hirohito had renounced his divinity—forever altering Japan's political future.

View of upper story bedroom occupied by General Douglas MacArthur, 1945–1951.

Residence
HABIB HOUSE
1976
Zo Za Young and
 Oudens + Knoop
Architects

SEOUL OLD AMERICAN LEGATION

The Seoul Old American Legation, built in 1883, is an exceptionally well preserved example of traditional Korean residential architecture. Lucius Foote, the first resident envoy from the West to arrive in Korea, purchased this picturesque house one year after its construction. Among the first American legations in the world, this house has been in the possession of the U.S. government longer than any other residence. It also holds the distinction of being the first among foreign legation offices to be built within the grounds of Korea's royal palace. Originally serving as both home and office of America's representative, it has been acknowledged by the Korean people as a symbol of freedom against aggressors. Situated at the entrance to the ambassador's current residence, the Seoul Old American Legation is recognized by both America and Korea as a symbol of the two countries' enduring diplomatic relationship.

Freedom is not free.

—Anonymous
Inscription on
Korean War Memorial
Washington, D.C.
Dedicated July 1995

Chancery &
    Residential Compound
1980
Ulaanbaatar City Building Office
Architects

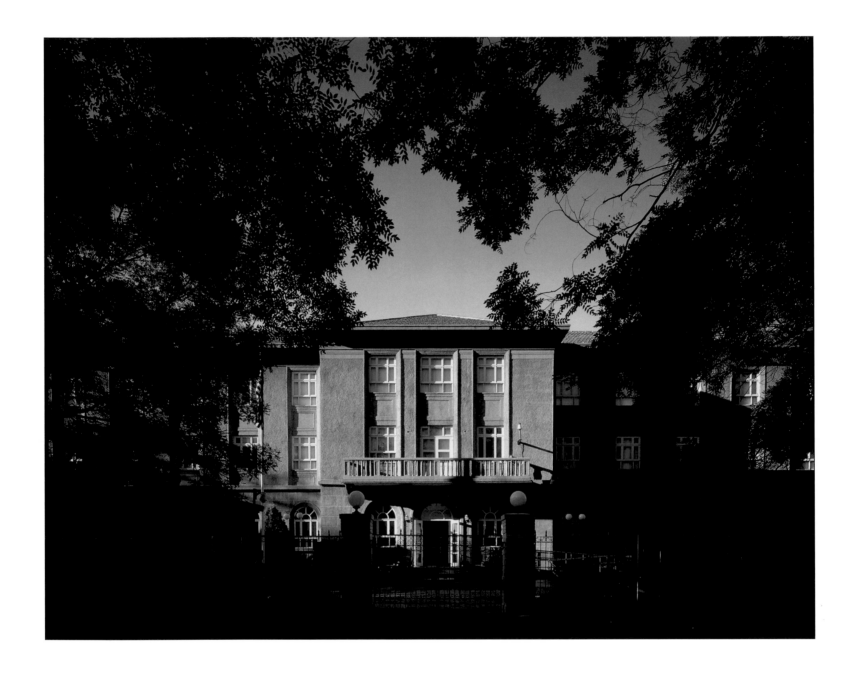

Chancery & Annexes
SAN BAN and ER BAN Compounds
1955
Bureau of the Ministry of Architectural
    Engineering of the PRC State Central
    Government and City Architectural
    Design Institute

Consulate General
1921
Regional architect

It is not our affluence or our plumbing, or our clogged freeways that grip the imagination of others. Rather it is the values upon which our system is built. These values imply our adherence not only to liberty and individual freedom, but also to international peace, law and order and constructive social purpose. When we depart from these values, we do so at our peril.

—Senator J. William Fulbright
(1905–1995)

Plaque reads, "This flag flew over the U.S. Consulate when it closed in May 1950."

Chancery Annex
1959
Alfred L. Aydelott
Architect

Residence
1910
M. La Collonge
Architect

Peace is a daily, a weekly, a monthly process, gradually changing opinions, slowly eroding old barriers, quietly building new structures.

—John Fitzgerald Kennedy
United Nations General Assembly
September 1963

Chancery
1926
Regional architect

Residence
TIGHNAMARA
1930
Regional architect
Built for McGregor and
    Company Teak Exporters

Chancery
1996
Kallmann, McKinnell & Wood
Architects

Chancery
1996
Kallmann, McKinnell & Wood
Architects

Residence
1914
Horacion Victor Bailey
Architect

Chancery
1958
Raymond & Rado
Architects

Residence
1928
Regional architect

Chancery
1983
Hartman-Cox
Architects

Residence
1923
Regional architect

Chancery
1997
The Stubbins Associates
Architects

Residence
1997
The Stubbins Associates
Architects

Chancery
1946
Office of Foreign Buildings Operations,
  U.S. Department of State

U.S. EMBASSY CANBERRA

The first U.S. ship to enter an Australian port was the *Philadelphia*, which arrived in Sydney in 1792. Increased commercial exchange continued throughout the nineteenth century, accelerating dramatically during the Gold Rush of the 1850s.

U.S. consular representation was gradually expanded, but official diplomatic relations, which had previously been conducted through the Government of the United Kingdom, were not established until January 1940. In July 1946 the rank of representatives exchanged by the two countries was raised to that of ambassador. The U.S. Embassy was the first embassy to be established in Canberra.

The State Department's Office of Foreign Buildings Operations chose to model the design of Canberra's chancery and residence on seventeenth-century Georgian-style architecture. Reflective of the colonial architecture of Thomas Jefferson, the buildings were inspired by those designed by Christopher Wren for Williamsburg, the capital of the Colony of Virginia from 1699 to 1779. This approach to embassy design in Canberra established a precedent by which other nations, following the United States' example, designed their embassies in historically traditional styles representative of their home country.

Most of the bricks used in the construction in the 1940s were kilned in Canberra, but additional bricks from the same source were not available in 1959 when it became necessary to expand the chancery. When an exhaustive search made it evident that it would not be possible to match the original bricks in Australia, it became necessary to obtain matching bricks from the United States from a source near Williamsburg. As the buildings stand today, the embassy is a blending of Australian and American materials and craftsmanship.

Residence
1945
Office of Foreign Buildings Operations,
U.S. Department of State

Europe

featuring

Reykjavík, Iceland

London, United Kingdom

Paris, France

The Hague, Netherlands

Moscow, Russia

Prague, Czech Republic

Zagreb, Croatia

Madrid, Spain

Rome, Italy

Athens, Greece

It isn't enough to talk about peace. One must believe in it.
And it isn't enough to believe in it. One must work at it.

—Eleanor Roosevelt
Voice of America Broadcast
1951

Chancery & Residence
1941
Gisli Halldorsson and
    S. Thordarsson
Architects

Chancery
1959
Eero Saarinen
Architect

WINFIELD HOUSE

Winfield House, the residence of the U.S. Ambassador to the Court of St. James', is sited on twelve acres in the northwest corner of London's Regent's Park. Heiress Barbara Hutton built this country manor in 1936. On the recommendation of Lord Louis Mountbatten, Hutton hired the English architectural firm of Wimperis, Simpson & Guthrie to design the house. Hutton named the red brick Georgian-style residence after her grandfather, F. W. (Winfield) Woolworth, who had founded the stores that bear his name. During World War II Winfield House was used as a Royal Air Force officers' club and then as a convalescent home for Canadian servicemen. After the war Hutton offered it to the U.S. government, to be used as the ambassador's residence, for the price of one American dollar.

The residence is among the properties that comprise the Regent's Park historic district established by the commissioners for the Crown Estate. Although Winfield House was built in the twentieth century, much of the interior—furniture, fireplaces, French paneling, Chinese hand-painted wallpaper found in an Irish castle—is eighteenth century. Its twelve-acre private garden within the city limits of London is second in size only to that of Buckingham Palace. In the early 1970s Ambassador and Mrs. Walter H. Annenberg generously supported the extensive redecoration of the residence, restoring its original grandeur. In 1999 FBO completed a comprehensive restoration of the residence. Winfield House continues to stand as a tangible symbol of the uniquely close relationship that exists between the United States and the United Kingdom.

Residence
WINFIELD HOUSE
1937
Wimperis, Simpson & Guthrie
Architects

Chancery Annex
Hôtel de Talleyrand
1767
Jean-François Chalgrin and
   Jacques-Ange Gabriel
Architects

Hôtel de Talleyrand

Hôtel de Talleyrand is a superb example of eighteenth-century French architecture and is a monument to European and American political and social history. The Hôtel's neoclassical design represents collaboration between Jacques-Ange Gabriel and Jean-François Chalgrin. Chalgrin, who was also the architect of the Arc de Triomphe, designed the entrance-court wall and the interior. The limestone exterior is a significant component of Gabriel's grand urban scheme for the Place Louis XV, now called the Place de la Concorde. The exterior is protected by the Monuments Historiques et Bâtiments de France.

Shortly after the establishment of the First Republic, this mansion became the residence of the French statesman Charles Maurice de Talleyrand, who as Minister of Foreign Affairs, plotted Napoleon's foreign policy and ultimately his fate. During World War II the Vichy government requisitioned the residence, as did the Germans following the fall of France. For their historical value, bullet holes in the façade were purposely left ragged, and in the basement detention cells are still ominously labeled with Nazi insignia. Purchased from Baron Guy de Rothschild after the war by the U.S. government, the building served as headquarters for the Marshall Plan.

The Hôtel de Talleyrand is currently used for Consular Affairs, the U.S. Information Service, and several other agency offices. The first-floor reception rooms are used for cultural events, conferences, and other activities promoting closer ties between the United States and France. The George C. Marshall Center, currently undergoing extensive historic restoration, occupies eleven rooms on the second floor, including the Harriman Chamber, honoring Ambassador Avril Harriman, who served from 1948 to 1950 as the Special Representative in Europe for the European Recovery Program. Once restored, this center will provide a stunning setting for diplomatic events and meetings for international scholars, artists, and leaders of government and business.

Residence
HÔTEL PONTALBA
formerly the Rothschild Residence
1842
Ludovico Visconti, Architect,
   with the Baroness Pontalba

215

The last hope of human liberty rests on us.

—Thomas Jefferson

Chancery
1959
Marcel Breuer
Architect

Chancery
2000
HOK/Washington
Architects

Dale Chihuly, *Macchia* installation, 2000.
Blown glass. Gift of the artist.

Residence
SPASO HOUSE
1914
Adamovich & Mayat
Architects

SCHOENBORN PALACE

The U.S. Embassy in Prague's Schoenborn Palace has a long and complex history of adaptations, accommodating a wide range of royal, noble, and governmental owners. Five medieval residences and a malt house were combined by various owners in the early decades of the seventeenth century. The building's Renaissance past is preserved in the courtyard stair tower, the geometric stucco ceilings, and the entrance portal with its rough stone set in a diamond "bossage" pattern. It was the 1718 renovation by expatriate Italian architect Santini that defined the structure as we know it today.

During the year before the Republic of Czechoslovakia was proclaimed in 1918, Franz Kafka occupied two rooms "high and beautiful, red and gold, almost like Versailles" in the Schoenborn Palace. Carl Johann Schoenborn sold the property to Chicago plumbing millionaire Richard Crane, Czechoslovakia's first American diplomat, who in turn sold the property in 1924 to the U.S. government for use as an American legation. The view to the Schoenborn Palace gardens from the Prague Castle has been an important part of the city's character for generations. It has been said that the illuminated American flag, flying atop the garden pavilion, has provided the citizens of Prague hopeful inspiration during times of political oppression.

*Glorietta on hillside
overlooking chancery.*

PETSCHEK HOUSE

This elegant beaux-arts residence was built in the late 1920s by Otto Petschek, a wealthy banker and industrialist. Petschek, the ultimate armchair architect, gathered inspiration from his many visits to Paris and was closely involved in every aspect of the design, but he died shortly after construction was completed. In 1938 his surviving family escaped the Nazis with an hour's notice and eventually settled in the United States, Argentina, and the United Kingdom. For most of World War II the house was occupied by General Toussaint, the German military governor of Prague, and after liberation by Soviet and Czechoslovakian forces. It was leased as the U.S. Embassy residence in 1948 and was eventually acquired as part of a war reparations settlement.

The floor plan is arranged in a sweeping crescent that embraces a large, formal terrace descending to a lawn and garden. Petschek and his architects were heavily influenced by salons and museums in Paris, particularly the Musée des Arts Décoratifs and the Musée Carnavalet. The beaux arts and art nouveau interiors were designed by Jansen of Paris and André Carlhian.

Because the residence became a refuge for dissidents during the Cold War, Czech citizens consider it a symbol of American support for the anti-Communist movement. Dissident writers, poets, and playwrights like Václav Havel would be invited to dinners, receptions, and concerts, providing opportunities for otherwise illegal meetings on U.S. sovereign territory. Unfortunately, sanctuary ended at the gate, a lesson learned the hard way by Havel—a leader of the "Velvet Revolution" and first democratically elected president of the Czech Republic—when he was arrested two blocks from the residence on his way home from one of these events.

Chancery
2003
HOK/Washington
Architects

Chancery & Residence
1952
Garrigues & Middlehurst
Architects

Deputy Chief of Mission
Residence
BYNE HOUSE
1885
Regional architect

Palazzo Margherita and Twin Villas

Palazzo Margherita, the U.S. Embassy chancery in Rome, was designed by Gaetano Koch and built between 1886 and 1890 for Prince Boncompagni Ludovisi. The site itself is of significance, as it is where Julius Caesar had his summer palace and where, it is said, he entertained Cleopatra. The palazzo, later named after the beloved Queen Mother Margherita, who took up residence at the beginning of the twentieth century, remained the center of society in Rome until the Queen Mother's death in 1926. During Mussolini's dictatorship the spacious royal chambers were partitioned into utilitarian offices for the National Fascist Confederation of Farmers.

By the end of the war the U.S. government had acquired other royal residences in the adjacent Twin Villas for the first American legation in Rome. In 1946 the Italian government gave Palazzo Margherita and all the works of art it contained to the U.S. government in return for cancellation of its war debt. At the time neither administration was aware that among those statues was Giambologna's *Venus*, a masterpiece of Renaissance sculpture. Between 1949 and 1952 Palazzo Margherita was extensively renovated, and rooms were restored to their earlier grandeur. Restoration work unearthed two-thousand-year-old Roman Imperial fresco paintings preserved in an underground passageway, the conservation of which has been supported by the U.S. Department of State and the World Monuments Fund. The discovery of the frescoes adds to the truly historic importance of this diplomatic property for both the United States and Italy.

Chancery
PALAZZO MARGHERITA
1890
Gaetano Koch
Architect

Residence
VILLA TAVERNA
1576

Chancery
1959
Walter Gropius with The Architects'
   Collaborative (TAC)
Architects

Residence
1931
Regional architect

EPILOGUE

WALTER GROPIUS DESIGNED THE U.S. CHANCERY IN ATHENS, DEDICATED IN 1961, using the Parthenon as his aesthetic model. The chancery is a wonderfully modest modernist building of some of the last marble quarried in Greece before Italy took over the Hellenistic marble industry. As I write from my hotel room in Athens, the mystical vision of the Parthenon fills my gaze. Solidly rooted on the Acropolis, it powerfully exerts its enduring presence over the spreading urban density of modern Athens. Every time I have looked toward that immortalized hill, the color of the Parthenon has changed. Every shade of white to tan to gray has emanated from the mammoth columns that attest the endurance of both architecture and ideals. In Western civilization the story of Greece is as much a concept and a myth as it is an epoch and a place. Here in Athens the visitor comes face to face with the authenticity of this collective archetype. As solid as columns of marble, as permanent as a mountain of stone, as awesome as the perfection of geometry, this mighty palace makes so very real the importance of ideas and truths that last. The Greece of today is not the one preserved in its philosophy and drama and mathematics. The democracy that ancient Greece immortalized, like any idealistic philosophy, exists in its purity more in the mythical realm of the past than in the complex geopolitics of the world today.

As I write the last words of this chronicle, I gaze at the great Parthenon, the seat of democracy, critical thought, justice, and moral humanism. The idealism of this enlightened civilization established the foundation of all modern democracies. Its culture, art, and architecture; its wisdom and judicious thought; its literature and drama; and its excellence, all continue to inspire the governments of free peoples. All this exists in our collective cultural memory, hovering like an allegory and reminding and promising us that what is most important will long endure.

Elizabeth Gill Lui
Athens, June 2002

Athens, Greece (chancery)

THROUGH THE MOVING LENS

As Elizabeth's partner in *Building Diplomacy*, my work consisted of filming the live-action documentary of the ambassadorial properties. Beyond that I looked deeply into the culture of the area surrounding each property.

Considering both the official representation of our nation through the architecture of our government's property and the unofficial representation of our nation through the cultural migration of commerce, entertainment, and style, this body of work, produced in collaboration, speaks deeply to the heart of American international identity. The images I have chosen to include in this book (which are available on DVD), contrast and complement Elizabeth's extensive work and, I hope, point to the broader cultural context within which our embassies stand. Our journey was as much about the why of diplomacy as it was about the what and the how. When one travels to foreign countries it becomes clear that the American flag flies in the presence of the world's diverse cultures, reminding us why employing diplomacy in all matters is an imperative. Our embassies are conduits of cultural communication and political exchange and are potential emissaries of a peaceful, integrated, and respectful world. An embassy is an outreached hand to those who want to build a relationship with a nation and the principles she stands for. Just as long ago Morocco reached out to Americans, validating our newborn cultural identity, we must continue to dedicate ourselves to living up to what we aspired to—both in 1789 and now—and to represent, throughout the world, those ideals: freedom of expression, freedom from want, and the undying need to share our culture, honor the other, and create a future. Together.

Keya Keita, Filmmaker
Los Angeles, April 2004

APPENDIXES

Seoul, Korea (residence)

APPENDIX C: ARTWORK IDENTIFICATION

Page 3 (Paris, France)
Lewis Iselin
Eve, 1968
Bronze

Page 28 (Buenos Aires, Argentina)
Decorative panel in French
19th-century manor style,
circa 1917
Oil on canvas

Page 43 (Ottawa, Canada)
Joel Shapiro
Conjunction, 1999
Bronze
Gift of Friends of Art &
Preservation in Embassies

MONTEVIDEO,
URUGUAY
Page 55, top
Ambassador Thomas J. Dodd
Western Landscape, 1990s
Fabric assemblage

LIMA, PERU
Page 63, bottom
Serena Bocchino
Love Field, 1994
Oil and graphite on canvas
Courtesy of the artist

MEXICO CITY,
MEXICO
Page 67
George Moore
The Place of Trees, 1997
Oaxacan tapestry

OTTAWA, CANADA
Page 71
Stuart Allen
Kite and Sailing Vessel, 1999
Suspended sculpture

Page 72
Frank Stella
Sunset Beach Sketch, 1967
Fluorescent and plain alkyd
on canvas
Gift of Friends of Art &
Preservation in Embassies

Page 74
Jack Harman
*Canadian Peacekeeping
Monument*, 1992

PRETORIA,
SOUTH AFRICA
Page 80
Koryn Rolstad
Untitled, 1992
Fabric assemblage by
Bannerworks

DAR ES SALAAM,
TANZANIA
Page 93
Bryn Craig
Montana Ranch, 2001
Oil on canvas

NAIROBI, KENYA
Page 98
Frank Andrews
Petroglyphs, 2003

Page 99, top (left to right)
Edward Curtis
Photographs, circa 1904
Pavel Tchelichew
Vase, 1939
Philippa Simpson
Glass Panels, 2003

Page 99, bottom
Nani Croze and studio artists,
Kitengali Glass Studio
Ngong Hills, 2003
Glass mosaic mural

MUSCAT, OMAN
Page 128 (left to right)
Jane Piper
*Flowers in Front of a Seated
Figure Gone*, 1989
Oil on canvas

Quita Brodhead
Dance of the Flowers, 1996
Oil on canvas

Bill Scott
Mille-Fleur, 1994
Acrylic on paper

KUWAIT CITY,
KUWAIT
Page 137
Dale Egee
Origin of Arabic Numerals,
1996
Tapestry
Philip Arundell, London,
Manufacturer

BANGKOK, THAILAND
Page 179, middle
John Nieto
Wild Horse, 1988
Acrylic on canvas
Courtesy Vetana Fine Art,
Santa Fe

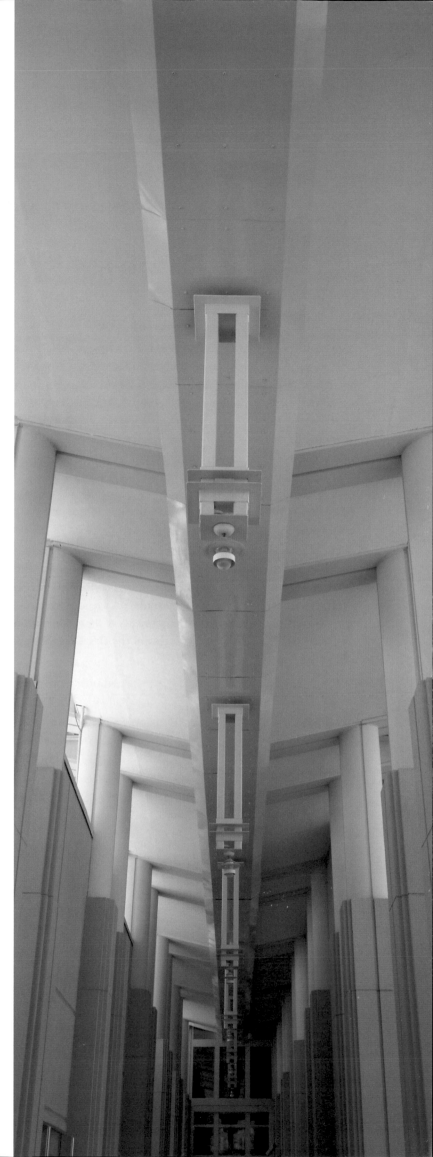

SINGAPORE
Page 193

    Gwynn Murrill
    Eagle, 1996
    Bronze

LONDON,
UNITED KINGDOM
Pages 209 and 210, top

    Antonio Berti
    Barbara Hutton, 1938
    Bronze
    Gift of the Price Foundation

Page 210, bottom

    G. G. Stapko after Thomas
    Scully
    Portrait of Thomas Jefferson
    Oil on canvas

    Suite of George III gilt wood
    furniture, circa 1790
    Gift of Ambassador and
    Mrs. Walter H. Annenberg

PARIS, FRANCE
Page 216

    Adolphe-William Bouguereau
    L'Amitié
    From the triptych *L'Amour,*
    L'Amitié, La Fortune
    Oil on canvas
    Gift of Mrs. Chester Dale

MOSCOW, RUSSIA
Page 221, top

    Pat Steir
    Carolina, Dakota, Georgia,
    2000 (three in a series of five)
    Oil on canvas

Pages 222–23

    Dale Chihuly
    Macchia Installation, 2000
    Blown glass
    Gift of the artist

PRAGUE,
CZECH REPUBLIC
Page 230

    Attributed to Albert
    Auwerrcx, late 17th century
    Brussels
    Tapestry depicting the
    mythological legend of Jason,
    showing Neptune inspecting
    the building of the *Argo*

ZAGREB, CROATIA
Page 235, middle

    Ivan Picelj
    Flag Variations, 2003
    Silkscreen

ROME, ITALY
Page 240

    Giambologna
    Venus, 1583
    Marble

Kuwait City, Kuwait (chancery)

A special thanks to Art in Embassies for first reviewing my proposal and providing an orientation to its valuable program of placing art in ambassadorial residences throughout the world. The Friends of Art and Preservation in Embassies has also contributed great art to many of our embassies around the world, and I would like to respectfully remember the former director, Lee McGrath, who gave so much to this important initiative.

I also thank Michael Boorstein and Robert Heath of the Center for Diplomacy for their interest and support. I wish them great success in achieving their goals of building a museum dedicated to telling the story of diplomacy and of building a public constituency for the same.

I am completely indebted to the staffs we worked with at each of our embassies. The hospitality of house managers throughout the world colored so much of our experience. The welcome cup of tea was always appreciated! In each country we had a control officer assigned to our project, and because of them, above all others, the work we were there to accomplish was facilitated and achieved. We worked with many fine Foreign Service officers from Administration, Facilities Management, Public Affairs and Public Diplomacy, Security, and the Motor Pool. By mentioning only a few I do not mean to do injustice to the high-quality support we received from so many people, Americans and foreign nationals alike.

We had the honor of meeting with almost every ambassador in the posts we visited, and we thank them and their spouses for allowing us access to their homes. Special thanks go as well to their staffs for their professional support and warm hospitality. To Ambassador Howard Leach in Paris I express my gratitude for his gracious accommodation of our work on September 12, 2001. For their personal hospitality I extend my deep appreciation to Ambassador Michael Rannenberger in Bamako; Ambassador and Mrs. Rust Deming in Tunis; Ambassador and Mrs. Craig Stapleton in Prague; Ambassador John Craig in Muscat; Ambassador Thomas Miller in Athens; Chargé Herbert W. Schulz in Singapore; Ambassador and Mrs. Paul Celucci in Ottawa; Ambassador Howard Baker and Nancy Kassenbaum Baker in Tokyo; Ambassador and Mrs. Jeffrey Davidow in Mexico City; Ambassador and Mrs. Robert Gelbard and their daughter Alix in Jakarta; Chargé and Mrs. Allen Nugent and their son Will in Palau; the William R. Stewart family in Muscat; and Chargé Heather Hodges in Madrid. Each in his or her own way took us in and made us feel less like wandering gypsies and more like American travelers being welcomed home.

Keya and I will always cherish special memories of the adventures we had with Will Steuer, Donna Roginski, and Sheila Malan in Pretoria; Thor Kuniholm at the American Legation Museum in Tangier; Rob Needham and Pamela Strangman in London; Harold Daveler in Lima; George Ibarra and Morris Williams in Mexico City; Jeffrey Hill in Muscat; Mr. and Mrs. Gale Ruff in Singapore; Judy Senykoff and Jeanine Jackson and the security office in Nairobi; Jacqueline Holland-Hart in Kampala; and Farida and Mark Strege in Accra. With the utmost respect we also thank the Security Offices in Moscow, Prague, Muscat, and Manila for their total professionalism and assistance.

As women traveling alone, we felt especially embraced and refreshed by our visits with Olga Iglina, Spaso House manager in Moscow; Chargé Priscilla Clapp in Rangoon; Alene Gelbard in Jakarta; Debra Smoker-Ali in Riyadh; Maria Paolo Pierini in Rome; Edith Gregorie Royall in Dar es Salaam; and Kristen Deming and Kathleen Stafford in Tunis. We shared poetry, painting, and culture, good food and enlightening conversation, and I thank them all for their friendship.

A contribution to the book's content on America's unique role in the history of Zanzibar was made possible through the assistance of historian and researcher John Baptist Da Silva, friend to many U.S. ambassadors and American visitors to Zanzibar.

And last but not least, I extend my respect and admiration to all the great Marines around the world who protected us while we worked and who do their jobs with the utmost professionalism.

Elizabeth Gill Lui

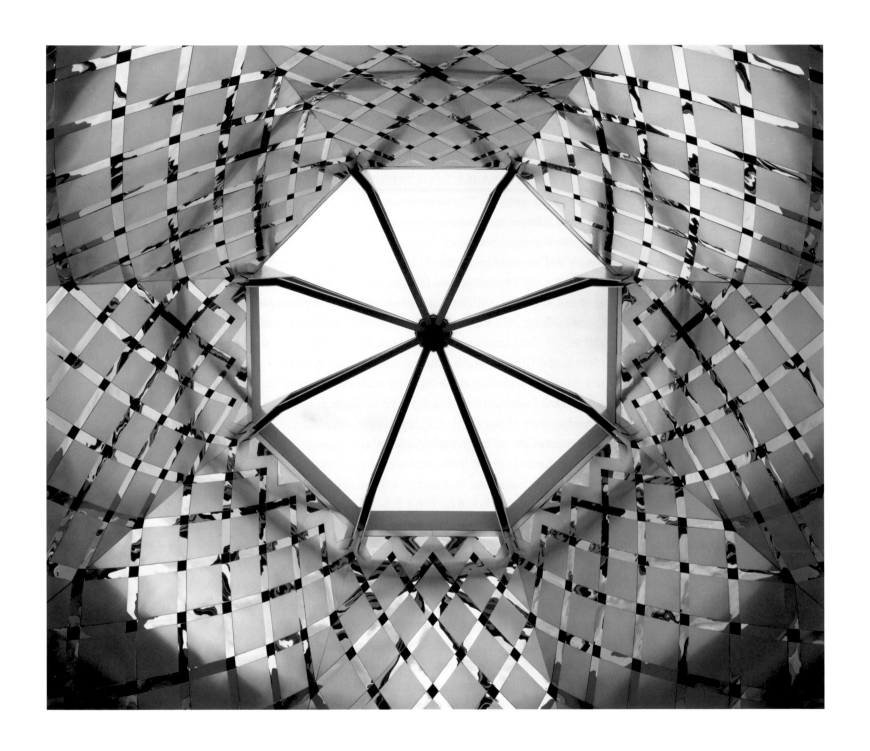

Ottawa, Canada (chancery)

ARCTIC OCEAN

Greenland
(DEN.)

Arctic Circle

ICELAND

U.S.

CANADA

UNITED
KINGDOM

IRELAND

NORTH
PACIFIC
OCEAN

UNITED STATES

NORTH
ATLANTIC
OCEAN

FRA

PORTUGAL   SPAIN

MOROCCO

Tropic of Cancer

Gulf of Mexico

THE
BAHAMAS

Western
Sahara

ALG

U.S.

MEXICO

CUBA

DOM.
HAITI REP.   Puerto Rico (U.S)

MAURITANIA

MALI

CAPE
VERDE

BELIZE   JAMAICA

ANTIGUA AND BARBUDA

GUATEMALA HONDURAS   Caribbean Sea

ST. KITTS AND NEVIS
ST. LUCIA

DOMINICA

SENEGAL

THE GAMBIA

BURKINA
FASO

EL SALVADOR   NICARAGUA

ST. VINCENT AND
THE GRENADINES

GRENADA

BARBADOS

GUINEA-BISSAU   GUINEA

BE
TO

PANAMA

TRINIDAD AND TOBAGO

SIERRA LEONE

CÔTE
D'IVOIRE   GHANA

COSTA RICA

VENEZUELA

GUYANA

LIBERIA

SURINAME

French Guiana
(FR.)

SAO TOME
AND PRINCIPE

COLOMBIA

EC

ECUADOR

KIRIBATI

BRAZIL

PERU

BOLIVIA

Equator

Tropic of Capricorn

PARAGUAY

SOUTH
ATLANTIC
OCEAN

SOUTH
PACIFIC
OCEAN

CHILE

URUGUAY

BOS. & H

C.A.R. -

ARGENTINA

CRO. - C

CZ. REP.

EST. - ES

F.Y.R.O.

LAT. - L

LITH. -

SLO. - S

SLOV. -

U.A.E. -

Antarctic Circle

Scale 1:75,000,000

Robinson Projection
standard parallels 38°N and 38°S